NEW CRAFTS

STICKS AND STONES

New Crafts
Sticks and Stones

Mary Maguire

PHOTOGRAPHY BY PETER WILLIAMS

LORENZ BOOKS

To the resurrection of Lowershaw Farm —
long may it prosper.

THIS EDITION FIRST PUBLISHED IN 1998 BY
LORENZ BOOKS

LORENZ BOOKS IS AN IMPRINT OF
ANNESS PUBLISHING LIMITED
HERMES HOUSE, 88–89 BLACKFRIARS ROAD
LONDON SE1 8HA

THIS EDITION PUBLISHED IN THE USA BY
LORENZ BOOKS, ANNESS PUBLISHING INC.,
27 WEST 20TH STREET, NEW YORK, NY
10011; (800) 354 9657

THIS EDITION IS DISTRIBUTED IN CANADA BY
RAINCOAST BOOKS, 8680 CAMBIE STREET
VANCOUVER, BRITISH COLUMBIA, V6P 6M9

ISBN 1 85967 616 2

A CIP CATALOGUE RECORD FOR THIS BOOK IS
AVAILABLE FROM THE BRITISH LIBRARY

PUBLISHER: JOANNA LORENZ
SENIOR EDITOR: LINDSAY PORTER
DESIGNER: LILIAN LINDBLOM
PHOTOGRAPHER: PETER WILLIAMS
STYLIST: GEORGINA RHODES
ILLUSTRATOR: MADELEINE DAVID

PRINTED IN HONG KONG

10 9 8 7 6 5 4 3 2 1

DISCLAIMER
The author and publishers have made every effort to ensure that all the instructions in this book are accurate and safe,
and therefore cannot accept liability for any resulting injury, damage or loss to persons or property however it may arise.

CONTENTS

INTRODUCTION

IN RECENT YEARS, OUR NEED TO FEEL IN TOUCH WITH NATURE AND CONCERNS FOR THE ENVIRONMENT HAVE LED TO A REVIVAL OF INTEREST IN NATURAL MATERIALS. STICKS AND STONES, THE HUMBLEST OF MATERIALS, HAVE BEEN USED SINCE EARLIEST TIMES AND STILL CONTINUE TO INSPIRE ARTISTS AND CRAFTSPEOPLE TODAY. WITH THESE SIMPLE AND READILY AVAILABLE MATERIALS, YOU TOO CAN CREATE FRESH, UNIQUE DESIGNS USING ONLY A FEW BASIC TECHNIQUES AND VERY LITTLE EQUIPMENT. THE 25 PROJECTS IN THIS BOOK SHOW YOU A WIDE RANGE OF IDEAS TO DECORATE YOUR HOME AND GARDEN, AND THE GALLERY OF WORK BY CONTEMPORARY ARTISTS AND CRAFTSPEOPLE WILL GIVE YOU FURTHER INSPIRATION FOR WORKING WITH STICKS AND STONES.

Left: Natural materials can be appreciated in their raw state or used as a basis for original designs.

HISTORY OF STICKS AND STONES

Stones are much more permanent than sticks and have given their name to the Stone Age, a period which dates back 2,000,000 years and lasted until 3000 BC. It is divided into three parts — Paleolithic, Mesolithic and Neolithic. At the beginning of the Paleolithic period, people were shattering and sharpening pebbles to make crude tools which slowly developed into axes, chisels, gaugers, borers and scrapers.

Pebbles have been collected and worn from the earliest times, sometimes perforated to make beads or coated in pigment. In 8000 BC, people in what is now France and Spain used red ochre to decorate hundreds of pebbles with dots, bars and wavy lines. Their use is not known but they may have been counters or tokens, or even part of a game.

Pebbles were also used to make the earliest known form of mosaic in Asia Minor in the 8th century BC. By the 3rd century BC, the Greeks were constructing huge mosaic pavement out of pebbles which were selected to achieve a subtle gradation from dark to light. In Macedonia mosaics reached a very high level of craftsmanship, with slivers of lead inserted into the mortar to outline contours and make figures stand out. Regional styles became distinctive, often incorporating bird, leaf or scroll motifs.

In ancient Chinese mosaics, geometric patterns were mixed with floral and free-flowing motifs, often outlined with roof tiles. Portuguese mosaics, by contrast, are usually bold and abstract. On the island of Majorca mosaics are divided into simple shapes outlined with cut stone blocks, which are then filled in with pebbles. In Spain mosaic paving is more refined, using grey, white and purplish pebbles to create a variety of geometric patterns.

Right: Pebble mosaic pavement from the gardens of the Alhambra Palace, Grenada, Spain.

Traditionally mosaic pavements were made by setting pebbles into a mud composed of sifted clay soil and water. The pebbles were set on end then pressed down into the mud until they were even. It is a craft that is regaining popularity and large pavements are being commissioned for public spaces in towns and cities.

As well as their functional and decorative qualities, in some cultures stones also have a spiritual significance. In Japanese gardens they are the foundation and the soul of the garden as they are believed to harbour the gods. A single stone may be the basis for the whole garden, and professional "stone-hunters" search the mountains to find stones of extraordinary character. These special stones are often placed in large areas of gravel, which is beautifully raked to give a feeling of serenity and perfect balance. Zen Buddhist monks incorporate this task into their daily meditation ritual, raking traditional patterns that have evolved over centuries.

Above: Many cultures made jewellery from stone, terracotta, shells and other natural objects. This stone necklace and bracelet come from Mali.

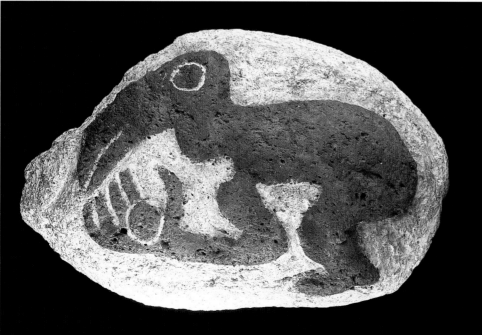

Left: . Boulder from the Easter Islands, painted with symbolic representation of a hybrid bird-man motif.

Sticks, being degradable, have not survived as stones have, but together with stones they were our earliest tools, weapons and building materials. Rubbing two sticks together first created fire, a fundamental step in human history. In AD 577 in China it was discovered that tiny pine sticks could be impregnated with sulphur and stored for later use. These "light-bringing slaves" evolved into matchsticks.

Woven together, sticks made an endless variety of useful baskets and containers for carrying and storing food. The earliest basket was probably a mass of tangled twigs which gradually developed into a woven form. Larger wattles and hurdles were used to make huts, fences and furnishing, and from the 12th century willow was grown as a cash crop to supply this market. The craft has never been mechanized and the same skills continue today, although much of the demand has been replaced by plastic.

By the Middle Ages woodlands were coppiced, which meant cutting them every few years to encourage the growth of fresh wood. Many types of wood were coppiced but the most common was hazel, which was used to make fences around sheepfolds, wattle panels for buildings and the hoops around barrels.

In the Far East, the earliest system of numerals involved five sticks laid on a table to represent the numbers 1 to 5. A stick laid at right angles across another five sticks indicated the number 10. Multiples of 10 were indicated in the same way.

Robert Louis Stevenson documented an interesting use of sticks in the Marshall Islands, a group of 34 widely scattered islands in the Pacific Ocean. The islanders developed a unique system of navigating, using sticks to make charts. Straight sticks indicated swells rolling into the islands,

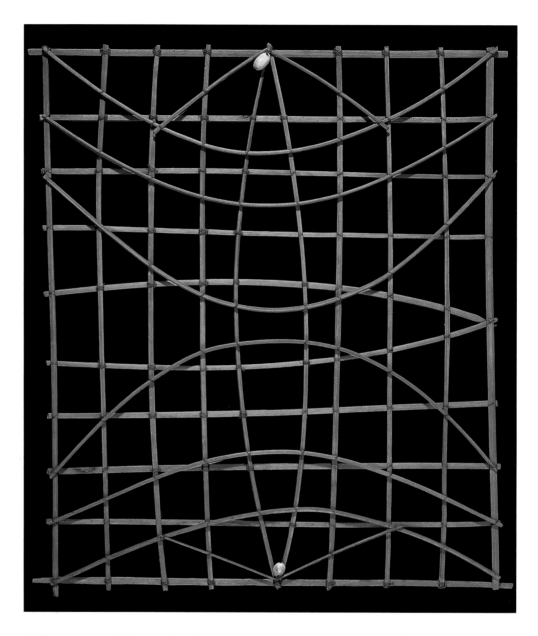

shells represented the specific islands and curved sticks indicated refracted swells of the sea.

One of the most basic uses for a stick is a walking stick, and all over the world people have whittled sticks of great diversity and ingenuity. Rustic furniture became especially popular during the Industrial Revolution in the Adirondacks area of America. Wealthy townspeople

Above: Sticks used to make a navigational chart from the Marshall Islands, as documented by Robert Louis Stevenson.

Left: The "Ideal Palace", Hauterives, France, created entirely from stones collected by Ferdinand Cheval in the late 19th and early 20th centuries.

Below: Ceremonial club, with carved head, USA. Native Americans made elaborate wood carvings for symbolic and religious purposes.

Bottom: Rustic bench, New Hampshire, USA, in the style characteristic of Adirondacks furniture of the 19th century.

yearning for a simpler way of life built lodges in the woods and on the edge of lakes where they spent their vacations learning to fish and hunt. The simple furniture fashioned by their guides developed into a booming business, and beds and chairs made of weirdly shaped gnarled branches became very fashionable. This furniture is once again being made.

Sticks and stones are cheap, accessible and easy to work with. They have always been used creatively by ordinary people, to make objects of practical everyday use or wild fantasies such as the designs of Ferdinand Chevel, a postman in Hauterives, France. His "Ideal Palace" was built entirely of stones collected on his daily round over 30 years from 1879–1912. This amazing achievement serves as an inspiration to us all. As one of the inscriptions in the palace states, "To the brave heart nothing is impossible."

GALLERY

I N ADDITION TO ECOLOGICAL CONCERNS, MANY ARTISTS AND CRAFTSPEOPLE ARE ATTRACTED TO ORGANIC MATERIALS FOR THEIR OWN SAKE. THEY RESPECT THE INTEGRITY OF THE RAW STATE AND NATURAL FORMS OF THESE MATERIALS RATHER THAN WANTING TO REFINE THEM, AND THIS SHOWS IN THE FINISHED WORK — SOME OF THE PIECES ILLUSTRATED HERE HAVE A QUIET, SIMPLE ELEGANCE; OTHERS A VIGOROUS SPIRIT FULL OF LIFE.

Above: STICK STOOL
This elegant stick stool is made of cultivated willow and coppiced ash. The intention is to achieve an ecological solution to contemporary design without imposing the artist's own identity on the finished product.
GUY MARTIN

Right: TWIG CHAIR
This chair was made by weaving and tying twigs together; then parts of it were stuffed with leaves and moss. These soft materials take on the character of the person sitting in the chair, and retain that character after they have left.
YVETTE MARTIN

Left: CANE BASKET
This basket is made of fine rattan cane, which is plaited to form the centre section. The border is twined and coiled with telephone wire, and the slate pebbles are drilled and threaded on to wire. The design is influenced by the collectors' cabinets popular in the 19th century, with each pebble separately framed.
DAIL BEHENNAH

Above: WILLOW FIGURES
Willow is readily bent and woven into many shapes, including sculptural forms such as oddly lifelike figures and animals or a giant "wave". Here the traditional techniques of working with willow, a renewable resource, have been used in a modern way that is still very much in sympathy with the material and with contemporary attitudes to the environment.
SERENA DE LA HEY

Below: CHEST OF DRAWERS
"The Ripple in the Water" is an eloquently descriptive name for this chest-of-drawers, made of softwood. It is carved, burnt, sandblasted, wire-brushed, sealed, coloured, burnished, waxed and, finally, buffed. The stones for the handles are gathered on beaches and are attached with leather thongs.
CARL HANS

Right: WILLOW FENCE
This fence, entitled "Fence at Ness Gardens", is 24 m (80 ft) long and is made entirely of willow, using 20 different varieties. Spirals, peepholes, bird nesting sites and willow animals are incorporated along the fence to give unexpected points of interest. It is made using traditional basket-weaving techniques.
STEPHANE BUNN

Above: PEBBLE DISH
The beauty of this piece lies in its simplicity, combining the natural colours and textures of the pebbles with that of the dish.
LOUISE SLATER

Opposite: BALANCED ROCKS
Brought down by the incoming tide, Talisker Bay, Isle of Skye, 11 October 1990.
ANDY GOLDSWORTHY

Opposite: BRANCHES
These branches were stacked
to form an opening into the
tree from which they grew.
Capenoch, Dumfriesshire,
January, 1996.
ANDY GOLDSWORTHY

Left:
ENVIRONMENTAL
WOOD SCULPTURE
This kind of scuplture is
not intended for gallery
exhibition, but for
people to come across
by chance when out for
a walk in the woods. It
is made of natural
materials found locally
and the inspiration is
largely dictated by the
spirit of the place. In an
outdoor setting vandal-
ism can be a problem
but the sculpture can be
recreated, perhaps even
in a new form.
BEN WILSON

Below and bottom:
STONE NECKLACE
AND BRACELET
This designer draws
inspiration from many
sources and many
historical eras. Here,
traditional African
jewellery was the
inspiration for these
striking contemporary
pieces.
ROMEO GIGLI

MATERIALS

STICKS AND STONES ARE EASY TO FIND — WHEN ON A WALK IN THE COUNTRY-SIDE OR BY THE SEA OR EVEN IN A TOWN GARDEN, LOOK OUT FOR NATURAL MATERIALS. STICKS CAN BE PURCHASED FROM FLORISTRY SUPPLIERS (SEE SUPPLIERS) AND STONES FROM BUILDERS' MERCHANTS OR GARDEN CENTRES. IF YOU ARE ON A COUNTRYSIDE FORAGE, HOWEVER, NEVER TAKE MATERIAL FROM CONSERVATION AREAS AND ALWAYS RESPECT THE LANDOWNER'S PROPERTY.

Aquarium gravel These small, smooth stones are available from pet shops and garden centres.

Bamboo Bamboo canes in varying sizes are available from garden centres and hardware stores.

Bundles of sticks These can be purchased from garden centres or collected in the countryside.

Bushel Even-length sticks can be purchased in this form if you are unable to collect them yourself.

Dried fruit It is easy to dry citrus fruits and apples yourself, or you can purchase dried fruit from a florist.

Fir cones These can be collected in pine woods in the autumn.

Hazel These branches are very flexible and are ideal for making curved shapes such as wreaths.

Moss Moss can be purchased from florists. Be very careful if you are collecting moss in the wild and only take a little from each area.

Pebbles These can be collected on beaches, or purchased from a garden centre or builders' merchant.

Pussy willow These attractive branches are available from florists' shops in the spring. Glue the buds to preserve them.

Raffia Natural colours are available from garden centres.

Red willow This is natural willow with the bark still on. It is available from florists' shops in the spring.

Semi-precious stones Stones such as agate and carnelian can be found on some beaches. Hold up to the light.

White willow withies Used in traditional basketry, these are willow stems with the bark stripped off to reveal the white wood beneath. They can be purchased by the bushel or half-bushel. Soak them in water before use to make them flexible, and do not allow them to dry out until you have finished working.

KEY

1 Pebbles	8 White willow withies
2 Semi-precious stones	9 Pussy willow
3 Aquarium gravel	10 Hazel
4 Bushel	11 Red willow
5 Bundle of sticks	12 Bamboo
6 Raffia	13 Dried fruit
7 Moss	14 Fir cones

EQUIPMENT

To make most of the projects in this book, you will need little more than glue and raffia plus the basic tools already in your toolbox. It is a good idea to invest in a good pair of secateurs (pruners) and a pruning saw if you wish to make several of the stick projects.

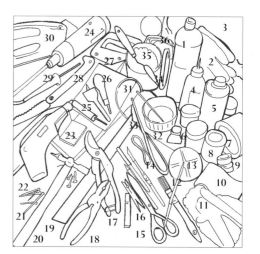

Artificial grass This is available from railway model shops.

Bradawl This is used to make a small hole to stop the drill from slipping. You can use another sharp instrument instead.

Brown aluminium bonsai wire This is available from garden centres.

Casein-based emulsion (latex) paint This paint is advised because it adheres best to the surface of stones.

Clothes pegs Use for clamping small pieces together while the glue dries.

Copper fuse wire This is available from electrical suppliers or craft shops.

Craft knife A craft knife is often used with a metal ruler to cut accurately. Use a cutting mat to protect your work surface.

Galvanized garden wire This is available from garden centres and hardware stores.

General tools Equipment such as scissors, a stapler, pliers, a hammer, and a selection of nails, nuts and bolts will all be useful for creating the projects.

Hammerhead-action (heavy-gauge) drill This stronger drill is needed to drill through hard stones. Use a tungsten carbide-tipped drill bit.

Heavy-duty double-sided tape This strong tape is available from hardware stores and carpet suppliers.

Masking tape This is useful for temporarily securing materials in position.

Matt spray varnish This protects finished work. Use in a well-ventilated area.

Micropore (floral) tape This stretchy tape is useful for willow structures.

Mini drill A lightweight drill is easy to use to make small items.

Paintbrushes You will need these in various sizes to decorate stick and stone surfaces.

Palette Use a china palette to mix paint colours or an old plate.

Palette knife This flexible knife is useful when spreading tile adhesive.

Plastic sheet Use a cover such as a dustbin liner (trash bag) to protect your work surface.

Pruning saw This is a good investment if you do a lot of work with branches.

PVA (white) glue This versatile, multi-purpose glue is transparent when dry.

Re-usable putty This is used to hold sticks and stones in place while they are being drilled.

Rubber (latex) gloves Use to protect your hands when mixing two-part epoxy putty (see below) or cement.

Secateurs (pruners) It is worth investing in a good pair of secateurs. If your hands are not strong, a ratchet model will make cutting much easier.

Soldering iron This can also be used to burn patterns into bamboo.

Spade drill This type of drill is used to make large holes.

Tile adhesive grouting Pebbles can be embedded into this to create a mosaic.

Tungsten carbide-tipped drill bit These will drill through very hard stones.

Two-part epoxy putty This adhesive putty is often known as Milliput, and is available from craft suppliers, model shops and large hardware stores.

Wood glue This is a specialist glue used to join wood to wood.

KEY

1 PVA (white) glue
2 Rubber (latex) gloves
3 Plastic sheet
4 Wood glue
5 Matt spray varnish
6 Casein-based emulsion (latex) paint
7 Masking tape
8 Heavy-duty double-sided tape
9 Micropore tape
10 Re-usable putty
11 Two-part epoxy putty
12 Paintbrush
13 Palette
14 Craft knife
15 Scissors
16 Clothes pegs
17 Secateurs (pruners)
18 Pliers
19 Ruler
20 Hammer
21 Screws, bolts and nails
22 Mini drill
23 Drill bits
24 Hammerhead-action (heavy-gauge) drill and Tungsten carbide-tipped drill bit
25 Spade drill
26 Bradawl
27 Saw
28 Pruning saw
29 Soldering iron
30 Stapler
31 Galvanized garden wire
32 Brown aluminium bonsai wire
33 Copper fuse wire
34 Palette knife
35 Tile adhesive grouting
36 Artificial grass

BASIC TECHNIQUES

THE MAIN TECHNIQUES YOU WILL NEED TO KNOW ARE MAKING HOLES IN STICKS AND STONES, AND JOINING THEM TOGETHER. MOST OF THE STICK PROJECTS CAN BE SAWN WITH A PRUNING SAW. BAMBOO SPLITS EASILY, SO USE A FINER-TOOTHED SAW SUCH AS A HACKSAW AND CUT IT SLOWLY AND CAREFULLY.

DRILLING HOLES IN STONES

1 If you can scratch the stone easily, you will probably be able to use an ordinary drill bit. Hold it in position with re-usable adhesive.

2 For very hard stones, use a hammer-action drill with a carbide-tipped drill bit.

JOINING STONES TOGETHER

1 If the stones are smooth, you will need to key the surface. Wearing plastic gloves, mix some two-part epoxy putty. Press and scrape this across the centre of the stone with a knife.

2 Using a paintbrush and water, blend the two-part epoxy putty onto the stone then rough up the surface. Leave to dry. Repeat steps 1 and 2 if both stone surfaces need to be glued together.

3 Press a ball of two-part epoxy putty between the two stones, so that it is between the keyed surfaces.

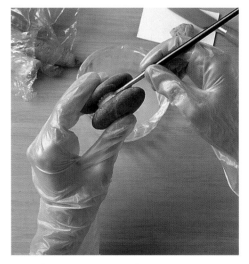

4 As you compress the two-part epoxy putty cracks will appear in it. Brush these smooth with a paintbrush and water.

MAKING STONE KNOBS

1 Find stones with a hole in one side. Press the head of a bolt or screw into the hole, using two-part epoxy putty.

DRILLING HOLES IN STICKS

1 It helps to hold small sticks in position on a wooden board, using re-usable adhesive. Make a pilot hole with a sharp implement such as a bradawl to prevent the drill from slipping. To drill larger pieces of wood, clamp them in position.

GRAFTING BRANCHES

1 Holding the branch in position with re-usable adhesive, drill a hole at the required point. Drill a corresponding hole in the branch to be grafted on.

2 Cut a straight section from a large paperclip. Glue it into the hole in the first branch. Leave to dry then glue the second branch on the end.

3 Wearing plastic gloves, mould two-part epoxy putty around the join to give a natural shape. Leave to dry then paint with matching ink.

SAWING POLES

1 A bench hook is very helpful for this. Nail a strip of wood along a sawn-off plank and hook this over the edge of your worktop. Nail another strip on the upper side of the opposite end, to resist the pole you are sawing against.

CANDELABRA

THIS FAIRYTALE CANDELABRA IS MADE FROM A TWISTED HAZEL BRANCH. YOU CAN USE A SINGLE BRANCH OR GRAFT ON EXTRA BRANCHES TO GIVE A PLEASING SHAPE (SEE BASIC TECHNIQUES). USE NON-FLAMMABLE INK AND POSITION THE CANDLE HOLDERS CAREFULLY SO THAT THE FLAMES WILL NOT REACH ANY OTHER BRANCHES. NEVER LEAVE LIT CANDLES UNATTENDED AND EXTINGUISH THEM BEFORE THEY BURN RIGHT DOWN.

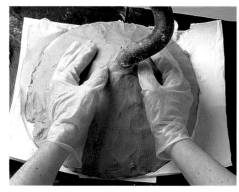

1 Protect your surface with a plastic sheet such as a dustbin liner (trash bag) and paper towels. Wearing rubber (latex) gloves, make a large mound of clay and embed the branch in it.

2 Leave the clay to dry for 2 days then place on a cake rack to allow the bottom to dry out. Wearing rubber gloves, spread the grout over the clay and sprinkle with gravel.

3 Press the gravel firmly into the grout evenly all over the clay.

4 Mix some two-part epoxy putty and roll into balls. Press onto the tips of selected branches. Using your thumb, shape into cups large enough to fit your candles.

5 Using a sharp stick, scratch vertical lines into the outside of each cup to give a rough texture.

6 Paint the cups with ink and leave to dry. Cut strips of foil and fold twice – they must be deep enough to line the cups to the rim, to prevent the edges from burning. Wrap each strip around your thumb and pinch it in at the bottom then smooth into the cup.

MATERIALS AND EQUIPMENT YOU WILL NEED

PLASTIC SHEET • PAPER TOWELS • RUBBER (LATEX) GLOVES • TWISTED HAZEL (OR SIMILAR) BRANCH • QUICK-DRYING CLAY •
CAKE RACK • TILE ADHESIVE GROUT AND SPREADER • AQUARIUM GRAVEL • TWO-PART EPOXY PUTTY • CANDLES • SHARP STICK •
BROWN WATER-BASED INK • ARTIST'S PAINTBRUSH • SCISSORS • ALUMINIUM FOIL

FAN ARCH

THIS STYLISH WILLOW TRELLIS IS EASY TO MAKE, ESPECIALLY IF YOU CAN LAY IT OUT FLAT ON THE GROUND TO STAKE OUT THE SHAPE. HELD TOGETHER WITH WIRE AND NAILS, IT IS STRONG ENOUGH TO SUPPORT CLIMBING PLANTS.

ALTERNATIVELY, YOU CAN LEAVE IT AS AN UNADORNED GEOMETRIC SHAPE, A STYLE OF GARDEN DECORATION WHICH WAS POPULAR IN FORMAL 17TH-CENTURY DUTCH GARDENS AND ALSO IN 19TH-CENTURY AMERICA.

1 Bind two pairs of willow stems together with wire. Bend to form two arches, the tallest 168 cm (66 in) high and the inner arch 25 cm (10 in) smaller.

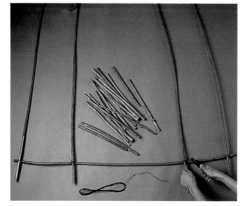

2 Cut two lengths of willow to fit across the arches as shown. Hold the spacing even by weighting the ends then bind the frame together with wire. Cut approximately 50 short willow sticks, 36 cm (14 in) long.

4 Using raffia, bind over the sticks in one direction as shown, then work back in the opposite direction to give a cross-stitch effect.

3 Drill holes in each stick 5 cm (2 in) from each end. Space the sticks evenly around the trellis in a radiating pattern and nail in place.

MATERIALS AND EQUIPMENT YOU WILL NEED

BUNCH OF LONG BROWN UNSTRIPPED WILLOW STEMS • GARDEN WIRE • PLIERS • PRUNING SAW • HOUSEHOLD OBJECTS TO USE AS WEIGHTS • HAND DRILL • HAMMER AND SMALL NAILS • RAFFIA • SCISSORS

BAMBOO CONTAINERS

THE HOLLOW SECTIONS OF BAMBOO CANES MAKE NATURAL LIGHTWEIGHT CONTAINERS, USEFUL FOR STORING PENS AND PAINTBRUSHES AND IDEAL AS GIFTS. DECORATE THE CONTAINERS WITH SIMPLE GEOMETRIC PATTERNS BURNT INTO THE BAMBOO WITH A SOLDERING IRON.

1 Saw off a section of bamboo above and below the joints.

2 Saw off 5 cm (2 in) from one end, for the lid.

3 Mark an even pencil line around the bamboo about 1 cm (½ in) from the cut end, use a saw to cut into this line without cutting all the way through the bamboo.

▶

MATERIALS AND EQUIPMENT YOU WILL NEED

BAMBOO CANE, APPROXIMATELY 10 CM (4 IN) DIAMETER • SAW • PENCIL • RIFFLER • ELECTRIC SOLDERING IRON • BROWN SHOE POLISH

4 Using a riffler, work evenly around the marked section.

5 Repeat around the inner edge of the lid, checking the lid on the pot as you work until you have a good fit.

6 Working on a protected or old surface, practise with the soldering iron on a spare piece of bamboo.

7 To create a chequerboard effect, rub the side of the soldering iron over the bamboo to make small black squares alternating with plain bamboo squares.

8 For finer lines, use the rim of the soldering iron. Finally, darken the ends of the container with brown shoe polish.

BEADED BOWL

THIS ATTRACTIVE BOWL, IDEAL FOR FRUIT OR PLANTS, IS SIMPLY MADE BY THREADING WIRE THROUGH STICKS. THE BEADS ACT AS REGULAR SPACERS BETWEEN THE STICKS, AND USING SMALLER OR LARGER BEADS WILL GIVE THE BOWL A DIFFERENT SHAPE AND CHARACTER. IF YOU CANNOT FIND BROWN WIRE, COLOUR GALVANIZED WIRE WITH A BROWN INDELIBLE MARKER PEN. A RUSH PLACEMAT FORMS A FIRM BASE.

1 Cut the sticks into even lengths, depending on the size of bowl required. Drill a hole 2.5 cm (1 in) from either end (see Basic Techniques).

2 Thread the wire through the holes at one end of each stick, adding a bead after each stick. Form into a circle.

3 When you have the required size, cut the wire. Twist the ends together so that there are no sharp edges and tuck out of sight. ▶

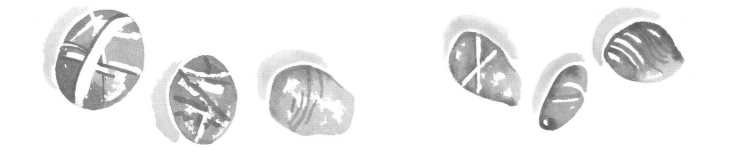

MATERIALS AND EQUIPMENT YOU WILL NEED

SECATEURS (PRUNERS) • STRAIGHT STICKS • HAND DRILL • BROWN GARDEN WIRE • LARGE WOODEN BEADS • PLIERS •
RUSH PLACEMAT • DARNING NEEDLE • FINE STRING • SEAGRASS OR NATURAL CORD • WOOD GLUE

4 Thread more wire through the holes at the other end of the sticks. Shape into a smaller circle, to fit the placemat. Finish the ends as before.

6 Stitch diagonally over each stick and through the placemat. Repeat in the opposite direction, stitching over the previous stitches to make cross stitches.

5 Place the placemat inside the bowl and stitch in place, using a darning needle and string. Check that the sticks are evenly distributed around the mat.

7 To strengthen the bowl, glue a length of seagrass or cord under the sticks and against the placemat. Leave to dry.

PAINTED PEBBLES

Collecting pebbles on the beach is a favourite pastime for any age group and painting them is just as satisfying. Look at each pebble carefully, noticing the subtle colours and markings, and try to work in harmony with them. Black, white, grey and ochre blend beautifully with the pebbles' natural colours. Use casein-based emulsion (latex) paints as these cling well to the stone surface.

1 Wear rubber (latex) gloves as the grease from your fingers may affect some pebbles. Draw your design in pencil then go over the lines in black paint.

3 Alternatively, paint the design in white instead of black.

4 Instead of highlights, add depth with pale grey and ochre. Finally, paint the details in black, using a very fine paintbrush.

2 Mix black and white paint to make shades of grey. Use these to highlight the design.

5 When the paint is dry, spray the pebbles with matt varnish.

MATERIALS AND EQUIPMENT YOU WILL NEED

SELECTION OF PEBBLES • RUBBER (LATEX) GLOVES • PENCIL • CASEIN-BASED EMULSION (LATEX) PAINT, IN BLACK, WHITE AND OCHRE •
MEDIUM-FINE AND VERY FINE ARTIST'S PAINTBRUSHES • CHINA PALETTE OR OLD WHITE PLATE, FOR MIXING PAINT • MATT SPRAY VARNISH

WILLOW LANTERNS

THESE MAGICAL LANTERNS ARE LOVELY FOR SPECIAL OUTDOOR FESTIVITIES, WHERE THE NIGHTLIGHT WILL CAST A LOVELY, SOFT LIGHT. TISSUE PAPER IS AVAILABLE IN A WIDE RANGE OF COLOURS AND CHILDREN WILL ENJOY MAKING THEIR OWN LANTERNS. WITHIES ARE SLENDER, BENDY WILLOW BRANCHES, STRIPPED OF THEIR BARK. BEFORE WORKING WITH THEM, SOAK THEM IN THE BATH FOR AN HOUR. DO NOT LEAVE LIT CANDLES UNATTENDED AT ANY TIME.

1 Take eight straight withies and tape the tips together.

2 Measure 86 cm (34 in) from the taped tips. Cut off the rest and discard. Tape the withies around a bamboo cane to form struts.

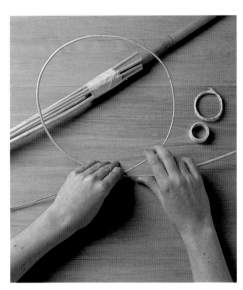

3 Bend two withy hoops, 25 cm (10 in) diameter and 5 cm (2 in) diameter, overlapping the ends. Tape the ends then cut off the excess. ▶

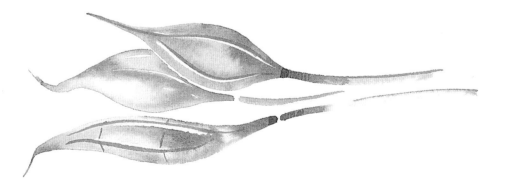

MATERIALS AND EQUIPMENT YOU WILL NEED
SMALL BUNCH OF WHITE WILLOW WITHIES • MASKING TAPE • TAPE MEASURE • SECATEURS (PRUNERS) •
BAMBOO CANE (AVAILABLE FROM A GARDEN CENTRE) • GARDEN WIRE • PLIERS • GLASS JAM JAR • LARGE SHEETS OF COLOURED TISSUE PAPER •
SCISSORS • PVA (WHITE) GLUE AND BRUSH • OLD BOWL, FOR MIXING GLUE • NIGHTLIGHTS

4 Push the large hoop into the struts, twisting it into a horizontal position once it is in the centre, then tape it to the struts. Remove the bamboo cane. Repeat with the small hoop at the open end of the struts, and also tape the withy tips together.

6 Place the jar in the centre of the frame. Attach it on either side by wrapping the wire around the withies at the junction of hoop and strut.

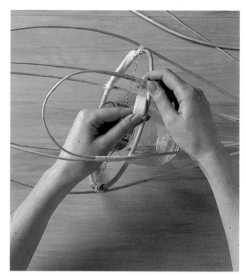

7 Bend an arch from a short piece of withy. Tape to one section of the frame as shown, to give access to the nightlight.

5 Using pliers, cut two pieces of garden wire and place either side of the neck of a jam jar. Twist the wires together to support the jar, leaving the ends untwisted.

8 Cut out petal shapes from tissue paper, slightly larger than each section of the lantern. Dilute the glue with water then brush onto the tissue shapes and withies. Fit the tissue paper in place, leaving the arch uncovered. Leave to dry. Place a nightlight in the jam jar.

LOG BOOK

THE DIFFERENT TEXTURES OF CORRUGATED CARDBOARD AND STICKS, HAND-MADE PAPER AND A RAFFIA AND PEBBLE FASTENING GIVE THIS WONDERFUL BOOK A TRULY ORGANIC LOOK, IDEAL FOR NATURE NOTES OR PRESSED FLOWERS. THE PAGES ARE SIMPLY HELD TOGETHER WITH A RUBBER BAND, SO YOU CAN EASILY REMOVE OR ADD INDIVIDUAL PAGES. AS A CHEAPER OPTION TO HANDMADE PAPER USE ORDINARY PAPER; INSTEAD OF CUTTING THE PAGES TO SIZE, FOLD THEM AND TEAR THEM AGAINST A RULER TO GIVE AN ATTRACTIVE ROUGH EDGE IN KEEPING WITH THE REST OF THE BOOK.

1 Using a craft knife and ruler, cut the cardboard and corrugated cardboard to measure 33 x 22 cm (13 x 8½ in). Cut the "moss" paper to measure 38 x 30 cm (15 x 12 in).

2 Score two parallel lines 6 cm (2½ in) apart across the centre of the cardboard, to make the spine. Stick double-sided tape outside the lines and all around the outer edge. Place the "moss" paper reverse side up and centre the cardboard on top. Fold over the paper around the edges and snip the corners.

3 Paint the corrugated cardboard with different-coloured inks, to give a striped effect.

▶

MATERIALS AND EQUIPMENT YOU WILL NEED
CRAFT KNIFE AND CUTTING MAT • METAL RULER • CARDBOARD • CORRUGATED CARDBOARD • MOSS EFFECT PAPER • HEAVY-DUTY DOUBLE-SIDED TAPE • SCISSORS • INKS, IN VARIOUS EARTHY COLOURS • ARTIST'S PAINTBRUSH • HANDMADE PAPER, IN CREAM AND RED • SECATEURS (PRUNERS) • ASSORTED THIN STICKS • WOOD GLUE • HOLE PUNCH • TWO PAPER FASTENERS • RAFFIA • RUBBER BAND • PEBBLE • TWO-PART EPOXY PUTTY • DARNING NEEDLE

4 Cut a small rectangle of cream paper, for the book title. Attach to the centre top of the book front with double-sided tape.

6 Using the point of the scissors, make two holes in the centre of the spine the same width apart as the holes in your hole punch. Insert a paper fastener in each hole.

8 Fold the sheets of red paper in half and punch holes in the centre of the folded edge. Insert the paper fasteners through the holes. Hold in place with a rubber band.

5 Using secateurs (pruners), cut the sticks to the length of the corrugated grooves. Glue in place, fitting them around the book title and leaving out the grooves over the spine. Leave to dry.

7 Wrap raffia along either edge of the spine. Tie the ends together inside the book cover.

9 Attach the pebble near the edge of the front cover with two-part epoxy putty. Using a darning needle, thread raffia through the edge of the back cover to make a loop to fit around the pebble.

RUSTIC PICTURE FRAME

INSPIRED BY DESIGNS FROM THE ADIRONDACKS, THIS GREEN AND TWIGGY FRAME WILL GIVE YOUR ROOM A LOG CABIN TOUCH. USE IT TO FRAME A PAINTING, A SELECTION OF PHOTOGRAPHS OR A MIRROR. A GROUP OF FRAMES COULD BE USED TO DISPLAY A SELECTION OF NATURAL OBJECTS. ASK AT YOUR SUPERMARKET FOR A DISCARDED FRUIT PACKING CRATE OR LOOK OUT FOR ONE IN A LOCAL STREET MARKET. ARTIFICIAL GRASS IS AVAILABLE FROM MODELMAKER'S SUPPLIERS.

1 Disassemble the packing crate, removing the staples carefully. Using a craft knife and metal ruler, cut three of the planks to the same size, as required for your picture frame. This frame measures 27 x 36 cm (10½ x 14 in).

3 Cut a piece of paper to mask off the required picture area. Coat the front of the frame with glue then sprinkle with artificial grass. Spread the grass out evenly with a fork then shake off the excess. Leave to dry.

5 Cut four thicker sticks to make a border around the outer frame, and four to make a border around the picture area. Tie together with raffia as shown.

2 Cut two small battens slightly shorter than the width of the frame. Staple onto the back as shown. Alternatively nail the battens in place and snip off any protruding ends with pliers.

4 Cut twigs approximately 11.5 cm (4½ in) long. Glue onto the surface in a diamond lattice pattern, using wood glue. Leave to dry.

6 Glue the two borders in position, using wood glue. Leave to dry. Insert your chosen image.

MATERIALS AND EQUIPMENT YOU WILL NEED

PLYWOOD PACKING CRATE • CRAFT KNIFE AND CUTTING MAT • METAL RULER • HEAVY-DUTY STAPLER OR HAMMER, SMALL NAILS AND PLIERS • PAPER • LARGE SCISSORS • PVA (WHITE) GLUE AND BRUSH • ARTIFICIAL GRASS • FORK • ASSORTED TWIGS AND STICKS • WOOD GLUE • RAFFIA

PEBBLE DRAWER KNOBS

DECORATE A PLAIN SET OF WOODEN DRAWERS WITH A LEAF DESIGN PAINTED FREEHAND IN SHADES OF GREY. FOR A HIGHLY INDIVIDUAL FINISHING TOUCH, ATTACH PEBBLE KNOBS PAINTED TO MATCH. BUY AN INEXPENSIVE SET OF SMALL WOODEN DRAWERS, OR RENOVATE AN OLD SET.

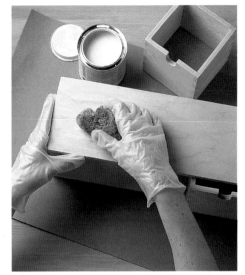

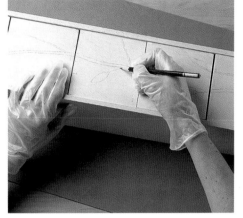

2 Draw a design of trailing stems and leaves across all the drawers in pencil.

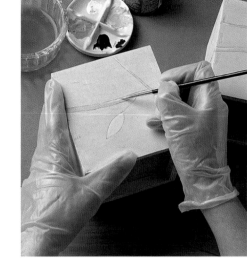

1 Wearing rubber (latex) gloves, sponge white wood stain evenly over the set of drawers. Leave to dry then apply a second coat. Leave to dry.

3 Mix the black and white paint to make several shades of grey. Using a medium-fine paintbrush, outline the design with pale grey paint.

4 Highlight the leaves and areas of the stems with white paint. ▶

MATERIALS AND EQUIPMENT YOU WILL NEED

RUBBER (LATEX) GLOVES • SPONGE • WHITE WOOD STAIN • SET OF WOODEN DRAWERS • PENCIL • CASEIN-BASED EMULSION (LATEX) PAINT, IN BLACK AND WHITE • MEDIUM-FINE AND VERY FINE ARTIST'S PAINTBRUSHES • CHINA PALETTE OR OLD WHITE PLATE, FOR MIXING PAINT • PEBBLES WITH A HOLE IN ONE SIDE (ONE FOR EACH DRAWER) • MATT SPRAY VARNISH • TWO-PART EPOXY PUTTY • SCREWS OR BOLTS (ONE FOR EACH DRAWER) • HAND DRILL

5 Use dark grey paint to give the effect of depth.

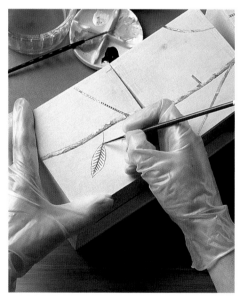

6 Changing to a very fine paintbrush, paint in the leaf veins and other details in black.

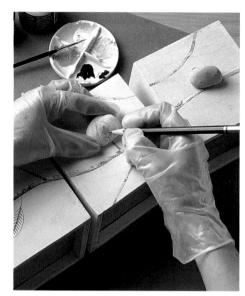

7 Hold a pebble over the centre of each drawer, where the knob will be attached. Draw a flower or other suitable motif in pencil to fit the design.

8 Paint the remaining pebbles with suitable motifs.

9 Spray the drawers and pebbles with varnish to protect the paintwork. Leave to dry.

10 Attach a screw or bolt to each pebble with two-part epoxy putty (see Basic Techniques). Make a pilot hole in the centre of each drawer then drill a hole and screw the knobs in position.

GARDEN TABLE

THIS STURDY TABLE IS IDEAL FOR EATING OUTDOORS BECAUSE THE WOOD IS ALREADY WEATHERED AND FURTHER AGEING WILL MAKE IT LOOK EVEN BETTER. YOU CAN LEAVE IT OUT IN ALL WEATHERS WITHOUT HAVING TO WORRY ABOUT IT. IF YOU WISH, YOU CAN PAINT THE FINISHED TABLE WITH CLEAR WOOD PRESERVATIVE TO LENGTHEN ITS LIFE. THIS TABLE TOP MEASURES 74 X 54 CM (29 X 21 IN), BUT YOU CAN ADAPT THE DESIGN TO WHATEVER SIZE YOU REQUIRE.

1 Saw the planks to measure 74 cm (29 in) long and lay them side by side. Cut two battens (laths) of wood 48 cm (19 in) long, drill holes then screw across the planks at either end to make the table top.

2 Saw the four poles into 91 cm (36 in) lengths, for the legs. Cut four sticks 43 cm (17 in) long

3 Nail two of the sticks a quarter of the way in from each pair of legs, to make side frames. ▶

MATERIALS AND EQUIPMENT YOU WILL NEED

FIVE WEATHERED WOODEN PLANKS, 15 CM (6 IN) WIDE • TAPE MEASURE • SAW • SPARE WOOD 5 CM (2 IN) WIDE AND 1 CM (½ IN) DEEP, FOR THE BATTENS (LATHS) • HAND DRILL • SCREWDRIVER AND 4 CM (1½ IN) SCREWS • FOUR ROUGH WOODEN POLES • LARGE STICKS • HAMMER AND NAILS • PENCIL • STRING

4 Lay the table top upside down. Centre the side frames on the battens and draw a circle around each leg in pencil.

6 Supporting the table top on a side frame, nail through the table top into the legs. Repeat for the other side frame.

7 Cut a thick stick 64 cm (25 in) long. Hold in place and nail it across the two side frames as shown.

5 Drill a pilot hole through the centre of each circle.

8 To stabilize the table, make a cross frame. Cut two sticks 91 cm (36 in) long and nail each from a front leg to the opposite back leg. Bind the sticks where they cross in the centre with string.

WEIGHTED TABLECLOTH

STONES AND PEBBLES MAKE PERFECT WEIGHTS, IDEAL FOR HOLDING DOWN AN OUTDOOR TABLECLOTH WHILE ADDING AN UNUSUAL DECORATION. DUCK CLOTH (CANVAS) IS AVAILABLE FROM ARTIST'S SUPPLIERS. YOU CAN ALSO TIE STONES TO THE CORNERS OF A COTTON TABLECLOTH FOR AN INSTANT EFFECT. STONES WITH HOLES ARE SURPRISINGLY COMMON, ESPECIALLY IN SOME AREAS. LOOKING FOR THEM MAKES A WALK ON THE BEACH EVEN MORE FUN.

1 Measure the table top and add 10 cm (4 in) all round. If the fabric isn't wide enough, pin two pieces with the selvedges together then machine-stitch.

2 If necessary, pin the seam flat and top-stitch.

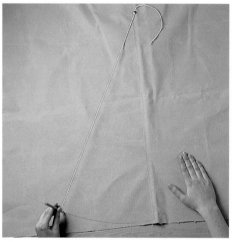

3 Mark a circle on the fabric by pinning a piece of string with a pencil on the end in the centre of the fabric. Draw a circle to the size required, keeping the pencil upright and the string taut.

4 Cut out the tablecloth. Pin and machine-stitch a small hem all round.

5 Mark even points along the hem for the stones to hang. Insert eyelets in the fabric at these points. Protect the work surface with a board under the fabric.

6 Hammer in the eyelets. Thread short lengths of string through the stones or pebbles then tie one through each eyelet. Alternate the stones along the hem to make the weight even.

MATERIALS AND EQUIPMENT YOU WILL NEED

TAPE MEASURE • DUCK CLOTH OR ARTIST'S CANVAS • DRESSMAKER'S PINS • SEWING MACHINE AND MATCHING THREAD • SCISSORS • DRAWING PIN (THUMB TACK), STRING AND PENCIL • BRASS EYELET KIT • HAMMER • BOARD • NATURAL STRING • STONES WITH HOLES THROUGH THE MIDDLE

STICK SPUTNIKS

THESE BIZARRE OBJECTS DEFINITELY LOOK EXTRA-TERRESTRIAL, BUT THEIR CORES ARE MADE FROM COTTON OR PAPER SO THEY SHOULD NOT REALLY VENTURE OUTDOORS, LET ALONE INTO SPACE. SUPPORT THE TWIGS CAREFULLY WHILE THEY ARE DRYING SO THAT THEY DO NOT BEND OUT OF SHAPE.

1 For each sputnik, cut the twigs into even lengths. Paint the cotton or paper ball with brown ink.

2 Make holes a little way into the surface of the ball, using a pointed implement. Work evenly all around the ball.

4 When the shape is complete, carefully push moss down between the twigs, to cover the ball. Repeat to make sputniks of different sizes.

3 Pour some glue into a bowl or saucer. Dip one end of each twig in the glue then into a hole in the ball. Complete small sections at a time and allow the glue to dry before continuing.

MATERIALS AND EQUIPMENT YOU WILL NEED

BUNCH OF TWIGS • SECATEURS (PRUNERS) • 7.5 CM (3 IN) DIAMETER COTTON BALLS OR BALLS OF PAPER • BROWN INK • ARTIST'S PAINTBRUSH • POINTED IMPLEMENT • PVA (WHITE) GLUE • OLD BOWL OR SAUCER• MOSS

DRIFTWOOD CUPBOARD

THE BLEACHED COLOUR AND TEXTURE OF DRIFTWOOD ARE HIGHLY FASHIONABLE NOWADAYS, ESPECIALLY IN A BATHROOM. THE CUPBOARD IS A PERFECT EXAMPLE OF THIS STYLE, AND USEFUL AS WELL. ADD TO THE SEASHORE EFFECT WITH A PIECE OF OLD ROPE AND A KNOB MADE OF STACKED PEBBLES. THE BACK OF THE CUPBOARD IS TREATED WITH A DISTRESSED PAINT TECHNIQUE IN KEEPING WITH THE REST OF THE FOUND MATERIALS.

1 Select similar pieces of driftwood 6.5 cm (2¾ in) wide. Saw two pieces 38 cm (15 in) long for the sides of the cupboard, and two pieces 16.5 cm (6½ in) long for the top and bottom. Sand any rough edges.

2 Arrange the four pieces of driftwood as shown to make a frame.

3 Drill two holes 9 cm (3½ in) apart in the centre of the top piece, large enough to thread the rope through.

MATERIALS AND EQUIPMENT YOU WILL NEED

PIECE OF DRIFTWOOD • SAW • SANDPAPER • HAND DRILL • SHORT PIECE OF OLD ROPE • SCREWDRIVER AND BRASS SCREWS • WOOD GLUE • PIECE OF HARDBOARD (FIBREBOARD), FOR THE BACK OF THE CUPBOARD • EMULSION (LATEX) PAINT, IN WHITE AND SKY BLUE • DECORATOR'S PAINTBRUSH • TWO SMALL BRASS HINGES • BRADAWL OR SIMILAR SHARP IMPLEMENT • THIN, SOFT PEBBLES • RE-USABLE PUTTY

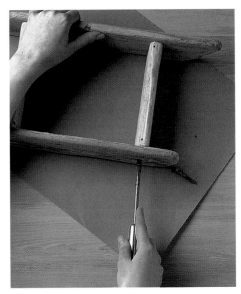

4 Drill pilot holes in the sides then screw the frame together.

6 Paint both sides of the hardboard (fibreboard) with white emulsion (latex). Leave to dry then paint with blue emulsion. When dry, rub with sandpaper to reveal the white paint in patches. Saw the hardboard to fit the back of the frame. Drill holes then screw in place.

7 Arrange various pieces of driftwood vertically across the front of the cupboard, for the door.

5 Glue the ends of the rope into the top of the frame, to form a loop for hanging.

8 Join the door pieces together with two battens (laths) across the back. ▶

9 Space the hinges evenly on the left-hand edge of the cupboard. Make pilot holes with a sharp implement then screw in place.

10 Lightly sand all over the cupboard. Mix a solution of salt and water and paint over the hinges, to give a verdigris effect in time.

12 Stack the pebbles on top of each other, with the largest at the top. Screw onto the centre right of the door.

11 Holding each pebble in place with re-usable putty, drill a hole through to take a large screw (see Basic Techniques).

COUNTRY CHAIR

RUSTIC FURNITURE IS VERY MUCH IN FASHION. THIS STURDY CHAIR WOULD LOOK GOOD EITHER INDOORS OR IN THE GARDEN. IT IS MADE USING BASIC WOODWORKING TECHNIQUES – WHEN YOU HAMMER IN A NAIL, MAKE SURE IT ENTERS THE CENTRE CORE OF THE POLE TO PREVENT THE WOOD FROM SPLITTING. USE POLES AND STICKS OF VARYING THICKNESS FOR THE CHAIR SEAT AND BACK, TO ADD EXTRA INTEREST.

1 Saw the poles into pairs measuring (A) 91 cm (36 in), (B) 68 cm (27 in), (C) 50 cm (20 in) and (D) 41 cm (16½ in) (see Basic Techniques).

2 Using a pencil, mark 34 cm (13½ in) from either end of poles A. Mark the mid-point of poles B.

4 Saw one 44.5 cm (17½ in) pole and one 37 cm (14½ in) pole. Join the side frames together with these poles as shown. ▶

3 Nail a pole D in place at the marked points on a pole A and a pole B. Lay a pole C across the top of pole B and nail together through the back of pole A. Repeat to make two side frames and arm rests.

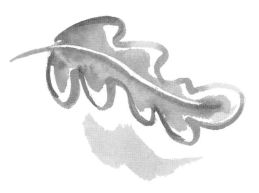

MATERIALS AND EQUIPMENT YOU WILL NEED

WOODEN POLES • SAW • RULER • PENCIL • HAMMER AND NAILS • HAND DRILL • HALF-ROUND POLES • LARGE STICKS • SEAGRASS, GARDEN TWINE OR STRING

5 Saw three poles 63.5 cm (25 in), 45 cm (17¾ in) and 44.5 cm (17½ in). Mark 15 cm (6 in) from each end of the first pole. Drill through these points then nail through them across the top of the chair. Bend the other two poles. Nail the second pole under the arm rests as shown, and the third under the front bar of the chair.

6 Saw half-round poles to fit across the chair seat. Drill holes then nail in place on either side.

7 Saw a selection of sticks to fit in a fan shape across the back of the chair and nail in place.

8 Bind seagrass, twine or string around the top of each stick and the back pole, pulling it taut.

9 Work back in the opposite direction to create a cross-stitch effect.

10 Wind the seagrass, twine or string around each front arm joint as shown.

ROCK POOL MIRROR

SEMI-PRECIOUS STONES SUCH AS AGATE AND CARNELIAN CAN BE FOUND ON SOME BEACHES. TO IDENTIFY THEM, HOLD THEM UP TO THE LIGHT AND THEY WILL GLOW WARM OCHRE OR DEEP RUSSET. ALTERNATIVELY, NATURAL OR POLISHED STONES ARE AVAILABLE FROM JEWELLERY SUPPLIERS. SCATTER THESE BEAUTIFUL STONES AROUND THE MIRROR FRAME, MIXING THEM WITH ORDINARY PEBBLES AND SHINGLE.

  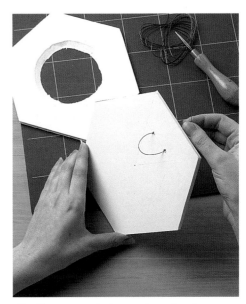

1 Trace the template from the back of the book, enlarging as necessary, and cut out. Using a craft knife, cutting mat and metal ruler, cut out twice from poly-board. Draw a circle 9.5 cm (3¾ in) diam-eter in the centre of one hexagon, using a pair of compasses (compass).

2 Carefully cut out the circle with a craft knife, holding the knife at an angle so that the hole has a sloping edge. Keep the cut-out circle.

3 Pierce two holes in the other hexagon as shown, for the backing. Insert a wire loop, to hang the mirror. ▶

MATERIALS AND EQUIPMENT YOU WILL NEED

TRACING PAPER AND PENCIL • SCISSORS • POLYBOARD • CRAFT KNIFE AND CUTTING MAT • METAL RULER •
PAIR OF COMPASSES (COMPASS) • BRADAWL OR OTHER SHARP IMPLEMENT • WIRE • PVA (WHITE) GLUE • 10 CM (4 IN) DIAMETER CIRCLE OF
MIRROR GLASS • MASKING TAPE • SMALL STICKS • TILE ADHESIVE GROUT • SMALL PALETTE KNIFE OR SPREADER • SMALL PEBBLES •
SEMI-PRECIOUS STONES • AQUARIUM GRAVEL • WATERCOLOUR PAINTS • SMALL ARTIST'S PAINTBRUSH •
CHINA PALETTE OR OLD WHITE PLATE, FOR MIXING PAINT

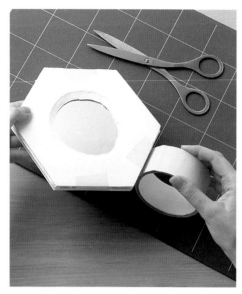

4 Glue the mirror glass circle in the centre of the backing, with the wire loop on the back. Place the other hexagon right side up on top to form a sandwich and tape together.

6 Replace the cut-out circle to protect the glass. Spread tile adhesive grout over the frame then arrange the pebbles and semi-precious stones on top, lightly pressing them into the grout. Leave to dry.

7 Remove the polyboard circle. Mix the aquarium gravel with PVA (white) glue and fill in the gaps between the stones, especially around the inner edge. Leave to dry.

5 Break or cut sticks to fit along the edges of the frame, overlapping them at the corners. Glue in place and leave to dry.

8 If you wish, add a second layer of sticks around the outside edge. Mix toning colours of watercolour paint with plenty of water and wash over the grout to blend it in.

MOSAIC SLABS

THESE LARGE-SCALE PEBBLE MOSAICS ARE VERY HARDWEARING AND CAN BE REPEATED AS MANY TIMES AS NECESSARY TO MAKE A PATH OR PATIO. THIS SLAB MEASURES 36 CM (14 IN) SQUARE — ANYTHING LARGER BECOMES TOO HEAVY AND WILL BE MORE LIKELY TO BREAK.

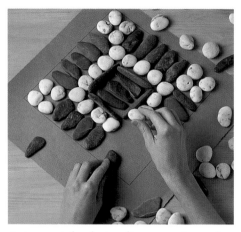

1 Lay out the design first on a piece of paper the same size as the finished slab.

2 Nail together the four pieces of wood to make a square frame. Cover the floor with a plastic sheet. Wearing rubber (latex) gloves, mix the cement in a bucket and fill the frame.

3 Press the cement down well, especially into the corners. Smooth the surface just below the top of the frame.

4 Transfer the pebbles from the paper onto the cement, pressing each pebble firmly in place. Leave for several days for the cement to set.

5 Remove the slab from the frame by banging the edge of the frame firmly on the ground. Repeat to make other designs.

MATERIALS AND EQUIPMENT YOU WILL NEED

SELECTION OF PEBBLES • LARGE SHEET OF PAPER • FOUR 36 CM (14 IN) PIECES OF 5 x 2.5 CM (2 x 1 IN) WOOD •
HAMMER AND NAILS • PLASTIC SHEET • RUBBER (LATEX) GLOVES • CEMENT • LARGE BUCKET

THATCHED BIRD HOUSE

COMPLETE WITH AN INGENIOUS THATCHED ROOF AND PEBBLEDASH WALLS, THIS IS A VERY DESIRABLE RESIDENCE TO ATTRACT NESTING BIRDS TO YOUR GARDEN. HANG IT OUT OF THE REACH OF PREDATORS. VARY THE SIZE OF THE ENTRANCE HOLE ACCORDING TO THE TYPE OF BIRD YOU WISH TO ATTRACT.

1 Trace the templates from the back of the book, enlarging as necessary. Wearing a protective face mask, cut out the shapes from MDF (medium-density fibreboard), using a saw.

2 Using a drill, cut an entrance hole in the top of the front wall as shown. Drill a small hole in the top of the back wall, to hang the finished bird house.

3 Glue the base and walls together. Hold in position with masking tape until the glue is dry.

MATERIALS AND EQUIPMENT YOU WILL NEED

TRACING PAPER AND PENCIL • PROTECTIVE FACE MASK • 6 MM (⅓ IN) THICK MDF (MEDIUM-DENSITY FIBREBOARD) • SAW • HAND DRILL WITH 4 CM (1½ IN) SPADE BIT • WOOD GLUE • MASKING TAPE • CRAFT KNIFE AND CUTTING MAT • METAL RULER • SELF-ADHESIVE ROOF FLASHING • RUBBER (LATEX) GLOVES • TILE ADHESIVE GROUT • SMALL PALETTE KNIFE OR SPREADER • AQUARIUM GRAVEL • WATERPROOF PVA (WHITE) GLUE AND BRUSH • OLD BOWL, TO MIX GLUE • FIBRE LINING FROM A HANGING BASKET • LARGE SCISSORS • RAFFIA • DARNING NEEDLE • CLOTHES PEGS • SMALL STICKS • WATERCOLOUR PAINTS • SMALL ARTIST'S PAINTBRUSH • CHINA PALETTE OR OLD WHITE PLATE, FOR MIXING PAINT • MATT VARNISH AND BRUSH

4 Using a craft knife, cutting mat and ruler, cut a strip of roof flashing the length of the roof and 13 cm (5 in) wide.

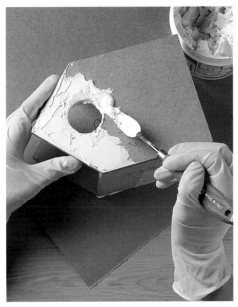

6 Wearing rubber (latex) gloves, spread tile adhesive grout over a small section of the front wall as shown.

8 Dilute PVA (white) glue with water and brush over the hanging basket lining. Leave to dry.

5 Tape the roof sides together. Peel off the backing from the roof flashing, centre over the ridge and stick in place.

7 Sprinkle aquarium gravel over the grout, placing darker stones around the entrance hole. Repeat until all the walls are covered with pebbledash.

9 Cut a rectangle 28 x 14 cm (11 x 5½ in) for the roof thatch and a strip 15 x 7.5 cm (6 x 3 in) for the ridge. ▶

10 Using raffia and a darning needle, make a row of large diagonal stitches along one long side of the ridge thatch. Work back in the opposite direction to make cross stitches. Make another row of cross stitches on the other side.

11 Glue the ridge thatch across the centre of the roof thatch. Leave to dry then stitch down the middle in running stitch.

12 Glue the MDF roof on top of the walls. Leave to dry then glue the thatch onto the roof. Secure with tape and clothes pegs until dry.

13 Spread grout under the eaves and along the front edge of the roof. Stick small sticks along these edges and leave to dry. Dilute toning colours of watercolour paint with plenty of water and wash over the grout to blend it in. When dry, apply a coat of varnish.

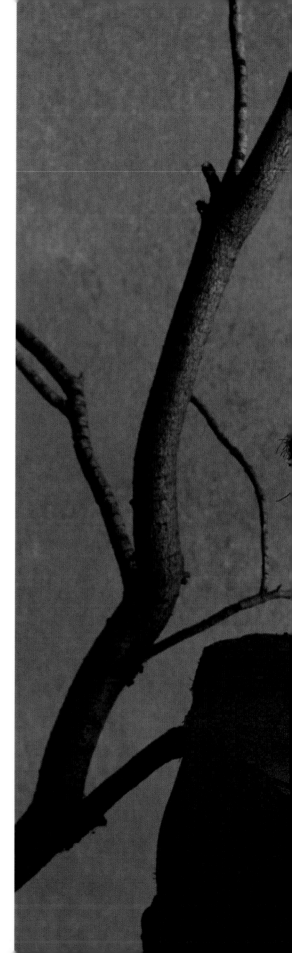

LEGGY LAMP

THE SCULPTURAL ELEGANCE OF THIS LAMP IS EASILY ACHIEVED WITH A TRIPOD OF INTERESTING STICKS AND STONE FEET. THE SHADE IS SIMPLY A PIECE OF HANDMADE PAPER WRAPPED INTO A CONE. CHOOSE PAPER THAT IS STIFF ENOUGH TO BE SELF-SUPPORTING — THERE ARE MANY TYPES AVAILABLE TODAY, INCLUDING THE ONE USED HERE EMBEDDED WITH LEAVES. ADAPT THE MEASUREMENTS IF YOU WISH TO MAKE A SMALLER TABLE LAMP.

1 Hold the sticks upright and place a rubber band around them, approximately a third of the way from the top. Arrange the stick legs into a tripod.

2 Place the end of each stick on a stone, adjusting the tripod as necessary. Key the surface of the stones then mould a "collar" around each stick with two-part epoxy putty. Carefully remove the sticks and leave the two-part epoxy putty to dry.

3 Glue the sticks into the two-part epoxy putty "collars". Leave to dry then bind around the elastic band with raffia. ▶

MATERIALS AND EQUIPMENT YOU WILL NEED

THREE SIMILAR STICKS, APPROXIMATELY 76 CM (30 IN) LONG • RUBBER BAND • THREE LARGE, FLAT STONES • TWO-PART EPOXY PUTTY • TWO-PART EPOXY GLUE • RAFFIA • SCISSORS • STRIPPED WHITE WILLOW WITHY OR 24 CM (9½ IN) DIAMETER EMBROIDERY HOOP • MASKING TAPE • WIRE • PLIERS • LIGHT FITTING (FIXTURE) (NB MAKE SURE IT IS EARTHED) • SHEET OF HANDMADE PAPER • DOUBLE-SIDED TAPE

4 Bend the willow withy into a hoop and secure with masking tape. Alternatively, use the inner ring of an embroidery hoop.

6 Using pliers, cut three lengths of wire and loop around the light fitting. Twist the wires together, leaving the ends open.

7 Twist the ends of the wires around the hoop, so that the light fitting (fixture) is suspended in the centre.

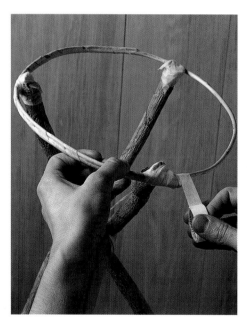

5 Tape the hoop onto the top of the stick tripod as shown.

8 Wrap the paper into a cone and secure with double-sided tape. Slide the paper cone over the hoop until it fits snugly. Secure with tape if desired.

WILLOW WALL RACK

FRESH UNSTRIPPED WILLOW IS AVAILABLE IN SPRING FROM FLORISTS' SHOPS, OR YOU CAN FIND IT GROWING NEAR A RIVERBANK. APTLY NAMED "WHIPS", THE STEMS ARE WONDERFULLY SUPPLE AND CAN BE BENT INTO MARVELLOUSLY FLUID, CURVY SHAPES. BEFORE YOU START, PRACTISE SNIPPING OUT A V-SHAPE AND BENDING THE WHIPS. USE THE RACK FOR STORING LIGHTWEIGHT ITEMS; ITS STRUCTURE IS NOT SUITABLE FOR SUPPORTING ANYTHING HEAVY.

1 Cut seven sticks 28 cm (11 in) long and five sticks 12 cm (4½ in) long. Drill pilot holes in two of each size (see Basic Techniques). Nail together to make a rectangular base.

3 Cut two 82 cm (32½ in) sticks and partially snip into the wood 1 cm (½ in) from each end. Measure and mark each stick into eight sections. Partially snip one side or the other at these points then bend the stick into a zigzag.

4 Bind the snipped ends of the zigzags to the corners of the base with raffia, so that they will lie flat along the long sides. Bind them to the base at all connecting points.

2 Glue the rest of the sticks on top of the base as shown. Leave to dry then bind together with raffia as shown.

5 Cut two more sticks 22 cm (8¾ in) and two 12 cm (4¾ in). Bind together to make a second rectangle, for the top of the rack. ▶

MATERIALS AND EQUIPMENT YOU WILL NEED

BUNCH OF FRESH RED WILLOW WHIPS • SECATEURS (PRUNERS) • TAPE MEASURE • HAND DRILL • HAMMER • SMALL NAILS • WOOD GLUE • RAFFIA • SCISSORS • MARKER PEN

6 Pull up the zigzags to make the sides of the rack. Lay the second rectangle on top and bind in place at connecting points, as before.

7 For the ends of the rack, cut two 40 cm (16 in) thinner sticks. Partially snip 16.5 cm (6½ in) from each end. Cross over and bind, as shown, then bind onto the rack at each end.

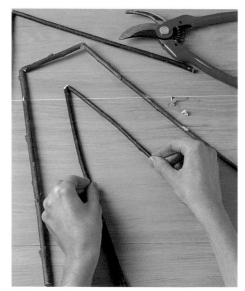

8 For the backing, cut three sticks and bend as shown. The top and bottom sticks are 70 cm (27½ in) and 67 cm (26½ in) respectively, partially snipped in the middle. The middle stick is 77 cm (30½ in), partially snipped 33 cm (13 in) from each end.

9 Bind together the three backing sticks as shown.

10 Cut a finer, very bendy stick and bind it onto the backing as shown to give it extra strength.

11 Glue the base and top of the rack to the backing. Leave to dry then bind securely together at connecting points.

BAMBOO WATER POURER

IN JAPANESE ZEN GARDENS, STICKS AND STONES HELP TO CREATE A FEELING OF PERFECT HARMONY. THIS BAMBOO DEVICE IS CALLED A "DEER SCARER" BECAUSE OF THE CLACKING SOUND IT MAKES. AS THE BAMBOO FILLS WITH WATER IT DIPS WITH THE WEIGHT, SPILLING THE WATER. WHEN EMPTY IT RISES AGAIN.

1 Saw an oblong piece 16.5 cm (6¾ in) long from the large bamboo cane, as shown.

2 Repeat on the opposite side of the bamboo.

3 Using a spade bit, drill a hole midway between the cut-out piece and the end of the bamboo, on one side only.

MATERIALS AND EQUIPMENT YOU WILL NEED

95 CM (37 IN) LENGTH OF 9 CM (3½ IN) DIAMETER BAMBOO CANE • FRETSAW • HAND DRILL WITH 2 CM (¼ IN) SPADE BIT • 2 CM (¼ IN) DIAMETER BAMBOO CANE • PLASTIC PIPE AND PUMP KIT • BROOM HANDLE • GARDEN TWINE • 4.5 CM (1¼ IN) DIAMETER BAMBOO CANE • 1 CM (½ IN) DIAMETER BAMBOO CANE • HAMMER • GURGLE POOL • GARDEN NETTING • GRAVEL

4 Saw a 15 cm (6 in) length of 2 cm (¾ in) diameter bamboo, for the spout. Saw off one end at an angle.

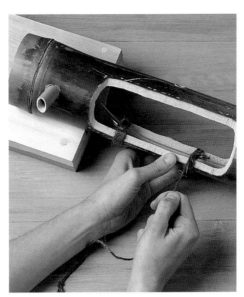

6 Wedge the plain end of the spout securely in the hole. Wrap garden twine around each end of the opening, as shown, to hold the pipe in place. Repeat on the other side for decorative effect.

8 Drill a 7 mm (⅜ in) hole through both sides of the large bamboo, to align with those on the tipper. Hammer the pin through the first hole in the large bamboo.

5 Using a broom handle, knock through the joints inside the large piece of bamboo. Thread the plastic pipe from the pump kit through from the bottom, out of the hole at the top then through the plain end of the spout.

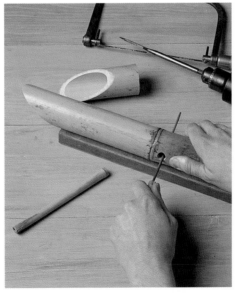

7 To make the tipper, saw a 46 cm (18 in) length of 4.5 cm (1¾ in) diameter bamboo, cutting one end at an angle. Drill a 7 mm (⅜ in) hole halfway along. Saw a 15 cm (6 in) length of 1 cm (½ in) diameter bamboo, for the pin.

9 Place the tipper through the opening, lining up the two holes. Hammer the pin through both holes. ▶

10 Fit the end of the large bamboo through the hole in the gurgle pool lid. You may have to enlarge the size of the hole depending on the width of the bamboo.

12 Stand the bamboo pourer into position. Insert the pump and place stones around it to support it.

11 Fit the pump to the end of the plastic pipe.

13 Put the lid onto the pool and pour gravel around to cover it.

AROMATIC CHRISTMAS TREE

STICKS AND DRIED CITRUS FRUITS MAKE A REFRESHING ALTERNATIVE TO A TRADITIONAL CHRISTMAS TREE. THE TREE IS TWO-DIMENSIONAL SO IT TAKES UP VERY LITTLE SPACE AND IS EASY TO MOVE AROUND. IF YOU PLACE IT IN FRONT OF A WINDOW, THE LIGHT WILL SHINE THROUGH THE FRUIT TO LOOK LIKE STAINED GLASS. YOU CAN BUY DRIED FRUIT FROM FLORISTS OR GIFT SHOPS, BUT IT IS VERY EASY AND MORE SATISFYING TO DRY YOUR OWN.

1 Cut two large sticks 100 cm (39 in) long and one stick 84 cm (33 in) long. Make a triangle with the shorter stick at the bottom, crossing over the ends. Tie together with natural-coloured raffia.

2 Cut another stick 134 cm (53 in) long. Tie down the centre of the tree frame, to make the trunk.

3 Using the thin sticks, cut pairs of graduating size to fit across the frame, with the ends protruding on either side. Tie one of each pair to the frame.

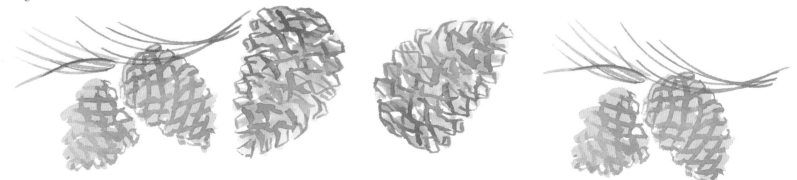

MATERIALS AND EQUIPMENT YOU WILL NEED

1.5 CM (⅝ IN) DIAMETER STICKS • PRUNING SAW • RAFFIA, IN NATURAL, ORANGE AND YELLOW • SCISSORS • BUNCH OF THIN STICKS •
HAND DRILL WITH SPADE BIT • LOG, APPROXIMATELY 20 CM (8 IN) DIAMETER AND 18 CM (7 IN) HIGH • ORANGES, GRAPEFRUIT AND LIMES •
SHARP KITCHEN KNIFE • GREASEPROOF (WAXED) PAPER • BAKING SHEET • FIR CONES • SMALL EYELET SCREWS • SMALL ADHESIVE PADS •
FUSE WIRE • WIRE-CUTTERS • PLIERS

4 Starting at the top with the longest stick, tie the other half of each pair of sticks diagonally across the frame to form a lattice.

6 Using a spade bit, drill a hole in the centre of the log large enough to secure the tree trunk stick.

7 Cut slices of fruit and place on a baking sheet lined with greaseproof (waxed) paper. Cut wedges from whole fruit as shown. Leave the slices and whole fruit to dry in a warm place or bake very slowly on a low setting in an oven.

5 Tie the sticks together at all the intersections.

8 Drill a pilot hole in the end of each fir cone and screw in an eyelet screw by hand. Thread raffia through the eyelet holes.

▶

9 Slice some of the whole dried fruit in half. Screw eyelet screws into the top of both the whole and the halved fruit.

10 Tie the whole and halved fruit onto the tree with orange and yellow raffia. Use adhesive pads to make the halved fruit hang straight.

12 Attach the slices of fruit to the tree, twisting the ends of the wire around the sticks with pliers. Hang the fir cones evenly along the bottom of the tree.

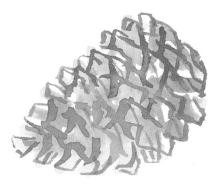

11 Using wire-cutters, cut short lengths of fuse wire. Thread one through each slice of dried fruit then twist together to make a loop for hanging. Leave the ends of the wire open.

STONE DOOR STOP

THESE STONE STRUCTURES ARE INSPIRED BY THE WORK OF ENVIRONMENTAL ARTIST ANDY GOLDSWORTHY. USE THEM AS DOOR STOPS OR BOOK ENDS, OR JUST AS BEAUTIFUL CALM SHAPES AMONG YOUR INDOOR PLANTS. CHOOSE STONES OF SIMILAR SHAPE AND COLOUR, THE FLATTER THE BETTER.

1 Lay out the stones in order of size. You will need about seven stones, depending on thickness.

3 Using epoxy putty, stick the largest stone to the board, for the base. Stick the other stones together in pairs, joining the keyed surfaces. Leave to dry.

5 Press aquarium gravel into the grout and leave to dry. If desired, wash over the grout with toning watercolour paint diluted with plenty of water, to blend it in.

2 Wearing rubber (latex) gloves, spread two-part epoxy putty over one side of each stone with a kitchen knife to key the surface (see Basic Techniques). Using a craft knife, pierce holes in the polyboard to fit the shape of the largest stone.

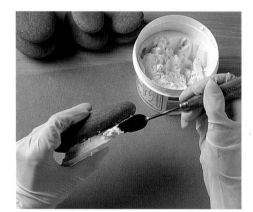

4 Lightly draw around the stone onto the polyboard and cut away the excess board with a craft knife. Using a small palette knife, fill in the gap under the base stone with tile adhesive grout.

6 Using epoxy putty as before, key the pairs of stones then join them together to make a tower. Press down firmly on top. Leave to dry, supporting the tower if necessary.

MATERIALS AND EQUIPMENT YOU WILL NEED

SIMILAR-SHAPED FLAT STONES, IN GRADUATING SIZES • RUBBER (LATEX) GLOVES • TWO-PART EPOXY PUTTY • KITCHEN KNIFE • CRAFT KNIFE • POLYBOARD • SMALL PALETTE KNIFE • TILE ADHESIVE GROUT • AQUARIUM GRAVEL • WATERCOLOUR PAINTS AND ARTIST'S PAINTBRUSH (OPTIONAL)

PUPPET HORSE

WITH A FEW HAND MOVEMENTS, YOU CAN MAKE THIS LITTLE HORSE TOSS HIS HEAD AND GALLOP AROUND. HIS SHINY CONKER (HORSE CHESTNUT) FEET GIVE A REALISTIC "CLIPPETY-CLOP" SOUND ON A HARD SURFACE.

THE ELF HAS A SEEDPOD HEAD GLUED ONTO A FIR CONE BODY, WITH A STRING GLUED AROUND THE TOP OF HIS HEAD TO OPERATE HIM. THE ARMS AND LEGS ARE MADE OF STRING AND BEADS, AND THE FEET ARE MADE OF CONKERS.

1 Cut a 60 cm (24 in) piece of natural-coloured string and several pieces 16 cm (6½ in) long. Loop the long piece around the centre of the shorter pieces of string, to make the tail.

2 Cut a bunch of twigs approximately 22 cm (8½ in) long then place them on a strip of double-sided tape. Lay the long tail string down the centre. Cut two 22 cm (8½ in) pieces of string and lay at right angles across the sticks, for the legs.

3 Roll up the bunch of twigs, wrapping the tape tightly around the centre. Cover the tape with raffia.

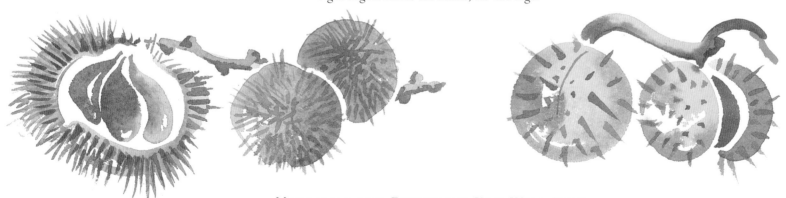

MATERIALS AND EQUIPMENT YOU WILL NEED

STRING, IN NATURAL AND BLUE • SCISSORS • BUNDLE OF TWIGS • SECATEURS (PRUNERS) • DOUBLE-SIDED TAPE •
RAFFIA • RUBBER BAND • FINE WIRE • WIRE-CUTTERS • DARNING NEEDLE • TWO SMALL WOODEN BEADS •
FOUR SMALL CONKERS (HORSE CHESTNUTS) • SKEWER OR OTHER SHARP IMPLEMENT

4 Cut a small bunch of short sticks for the head. Using a rubber band, bind one end onto one of the long strings extending from the head end of the body. Allow 7 cm (2¾ in) of string for the neck.

6 Flatten the top of the head and bind with wire.

7 Again allowing 7 cm (2¾ in) for the neck, wrap the second string over the wire. Tie the end.

5 Wind the extra string extending from the nose around the nose, to make a muzzle. Tie the end.

8 Make loops of raffia over both neck strings as shown, for the mane. ▶

9 Cut two short pieces of blue string and knot each at one end. Using a darning needle, thread through a wooden bead. Attach on either side of the head, for the eyes.

11 Using a sharp implement, pierce holes through the conkers (horse chestnuts). Thread the ends of the leg strings through the conkers and knot. Brush the mane.

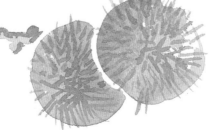

10 Cut a bunch of sticks approximately 21 cm (8½ in) long for the handle. Attach with short lengths of string to the head and above the tail. Bind the handle with blue string.

PUSSY WILLOW TRELLIS

EVERYONE LOVES THE VELVETY GREY BUDS OF PUSSY WILLOW AND THIS PROJECT SHOWS YOU HOW TO PRESERVE THEM AT THIS DELICATE STAGE. THE MAIN REQUIREMENT IS PLENTY OF SPACE TO WORK IN. THE TRELLIS IS DESIGNED FOR INDOOR USE, AS A FEATURE IN ITS OWN RIGHT OR TO SUPPORT POTTED PLANTS.

1 Place a small blob of glue on the base of each bud and leave to dry. Cross over the tips of two stems of pussy willow. Tie together with raffia to make an arch.

3 Weave the stems under and over to create a diamond lattice.

4 Tie the stems together with raffia at all the points where they cross.

2 Tie the tips of two more stems 10 cm (4 in) down from the point of the arch on either side. Cross the stems directly below the point of the arch. Continue to add more stems at intervals.

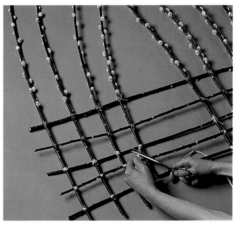

5 Tie sticks across the bottom of the trellis, to secure the structure and the spacing of the stems.

MATERIALS AND EQUIPMENT YOU WILL NEED
PUSSY WILLOW STEMS, APPROXIMATELY 140 CM (55 IN) LONG • PVA (WHITE) GLUE • RAFFIA • SCISSORS • STRAIGHT STICKS

TWIGGY WREATH

THE CIRCULAR SHAPE OF WREATHS REPRESENTS ETERNITY. FOR CENTURIES THEY HAVE BEEN HUNG ON FRONT DOORS AS A SIGN OF WELCOME. THIS SIMPLE, UNADORNED WREATH IS MADE OF YOUNG HAZEL BUT YOU CAN USE OTHER TWIGGY PRUNINGS — IT IS EASIEST TO WORK WITH THEM WHILE THEY ARE STILL FRESH AND FLEXIBLE. THE WREATH IS ROBUST ENOUGH TO HANG OUTDOORS ON A GATE OR SHED DOOR.

1 Bend half of the longer branches with your hands to make a curved shape.

3 Take a bunch of short twiggy prunings and hold firmly in one hand at the top of the circle. Using your other hand, wrap wire around both the prunings and the circle to join them together. Pull the wire tight.

5 Cut the wire and wrap round the wreath to secure the end.

2 Bend the same number of longer branches in the opposite direction. Place the two sets of curved branches so that they form a circle, overlapping the ends. Bind together with lengths of florists' wire.

4 Continue with the same length of wire, adding more bunches of twiggy prunings until the circle is covered. Check as you work that the wreath looks even.

6 Poke extra prunings at random into the wreath to give it more texture and hide the wire.

MATERIALS AND EQUIPMENT YOU WILL NEED

BUNCH OF HAZEL BRANCHES OR SIMILAR • REEL OF FLORISTS' WIRE • STRONG SCISSORS

TEMPLATES

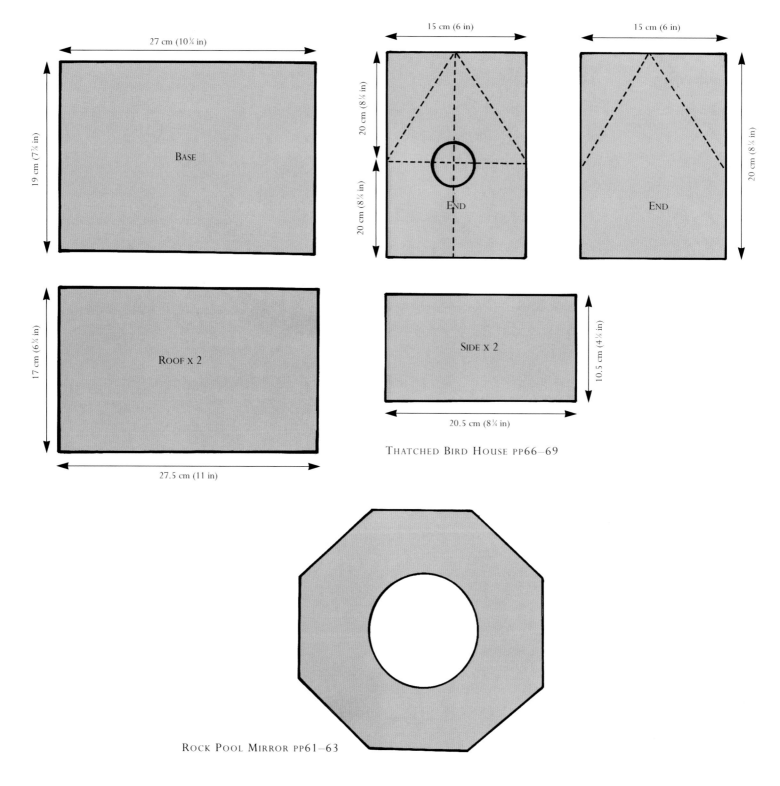

27 cm (10¾ in)

19 cm (7½ in)

BASE

15 cm (6 in)

20 cm (8⅛ in)

20 cm (8⅛ in)

END

15 cm (6 in)

20 cm (8⅛ in)

END

17 cm (6¾ in)

ROOF x 2

27.5 cm (11 in)

4⅛ in

SIDE x 2

10.5 cm (4⅛ in)

20.5 cm (8¼ in)

THATCHED BIRD HOUSE PP66–69

ROCK POOL MIRROR PP61–63

SUPPLIERS

Few of the materials used in this book require specialist suppliers; sticks and stones can be found in the garden, woods or by the seashore. (Do make sure you do not take anything from private property or conservation areas.) Most florists will stock a variety of natural materials, and many may be able to order what you require. DIY (hardware) stores and good craft shops should be able to supply the remaining items.

United Kingdom

The Cane Shop
207 Blackstock Road
Highbury Vale
London N5 2LL
(tel: 0171 354 4217)
(willow withies, bamboo)

European Bamboo Society
Morton
Bourne, Lincs.
(tel: 01778 837 546)
(giant bamboo stalks)

McQueens Flowers
126 St John Street
London EC1
(tel: 0171 251 5505)
(natural materials)

Paperchase
Tottenham Court Road
London W1
(wide selection of handmade papers)

United States

The Art Store
935 Eerie Blvd.
Syracuse, NY 13210
(tel: 315 474 1000)
(well-stocked art supplier)

Papersource Inc.
730 N Franklin Suite 111
Chicago Il 60610
(tel: 813 526 4880)
(wide selection of specialist papers)

ACKNOWLEDGEMENTS

The author and publishers would like to thank the following for contributing projects to this book:
Andrew Gilmore (Bamboo Containers, Country Chair, Bamboo Water Pourer); Emma Hardy (Weighted Tablecloth), Ercole Moroni of McQueen's Flowers (Twiggy Wreath); Helen Smythe (Painted Pebbles, Pebble Drawer Knobs); Wendy Wilbraham (Mosaic Slabs); Peter Williams (Garden Table)

AUTHOR'S ACKNOWLEDGEMENTS
Thank you to Peter Williams for his beautiful photography and Georgina Rhodes for her styling.
A special thank you to Andrew Gilmore for all his help and support

PUBLISHERS' ACKNOWLEDGEMENTS
The publishers would like to thank Minicraft, PO Box 16, Meadowfield Avenue, Spennymoor, Co Durham
D6 6JF (tel: 01388 423 115) for the loan of drills and attachments.

PICTURE CREDITS
The publishers would like to thank the following for additional images: Edifice Picture Lbrary: pp8 and 11 bottom right; British Museum: pp9 bottom, 10 and 11 top right; © John Bigelow Taylor: p9 top; Philip Reeve: p11 left; © Bill de la Hey: p13 top; © Jacqui Hurst: p14 bottom left; © Andy Goldsworthy: pp15, 16

INDEX